Creative Crafts for Children

Creative Crafts
for Children

Kate Pountney

Faber and Faber London

First published in 1977
by Faber and Faber Limited
3 Queen Square London WC1
Printed in Great Britain by
BAS Printers Limited, Wallop, Hampshire

British Library Cataloguing in Publication Data

Pountney, Kate
  Creative crafts for children.
  1. Handicraft—Juvenile literature
  I. Title
  745.5   TT160

  ISBN 0-571-10948-9

Contents

Introduction

This book explains many different ways of making things yourself. You will find that this can be an enthralling process: first you have to think up a good idea, then there are always problems to be solved, soon things start taking shape, and finally there is the exciting end result. Whatever you make will be special because there will be nothing else exactly like it in the whole world.

Find a clear work space, read through the instructions carefully and then assemble everything you need. Try to work with care and patience. If you rush, the result could be a badly made object that you will not feel happy about. If you have any difficulties remember that you can always ask parents or a teacher for some help; they would probably love an excuse to try out some of these ideas themselves!

Lastly, never be put off if a subject seems to have a lot of instructions. If you like an idea—then have a go. It is surprising how much easier things seem to be once you have started, and the subjects that require more effort at the experimental stage often achieve the most exciting results. Taking that first step could be just the beginning of a fascinating new hobby that will keep you absorbed through many dark winter evenings and rainy week-ends.

Tools and Materials

Most of the equipment that you will need for general craft work can be found at home. It is a good idea to start by finding a few basic items such as a sharp pair of scissors that is easy to handle, a ruler, a soft lead pencil, some paints, a couple of brushes including a stiff one for paper pasting, and some clean jam jars. More unusual things can be bought or borrowed as and when you need them. You can buy tools to fit your hands: a small pair of pliers is better than a pair you can hardly lift!

One very important item in your collection will be a large tube of all-purpose glue. It can be bought under a variety of brand names ('Uhu', 'Bostik' etc.) and is good because it sticks almost anything. Another useful glue is cold water wallpaper paste, which can be bought from a painting and decorating shop. Make up small amounts of paste when you require it, following the instructions on the packet, and keep the mixture in a clean screw-top jar.

Start a collection of materials, and store them in a giant cardboard box. Sheets of wrapping paper, pieces of card and interesting-shaped cartons can all be rescued from the kitchen before your mother throws them away. Cut out any pages from old magazines that have attractive patterns and colours; they will be good for collage decoration. Save old newspapers, string, scraps of material, and anything else that you think might come in useful. You never know, one day they might be just what you want.

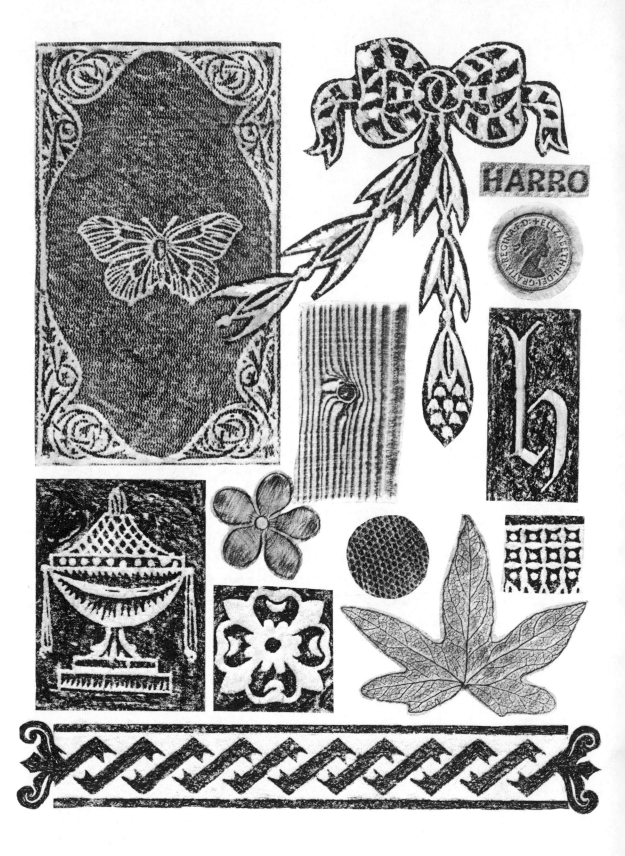

1. Rubbings

Have you ever put a coin under a piece of thin paper, and then rubbed a pencil over the top? The coin design appears on the paper as if by magic. Of course it is not really magic. If you look carefully at the coin, and rub your finger over it, you will find that it has a bumpy texture. Some of the pattern stands out from the surface forming ridges, whilst other parts are lower in the metal and become hollows. When the pencil is rubbed over the paper it catches on the raised surface of the coin and darkens these areas, but glides over the hollows, leaving them white.

Any fairly flat object with a textured surface can be used for a rubbing. Lots of suitable things can be found at home. A cheese grater, rough-textured material, tin lids and keys all work very well.

To take a rubbing you will need a sheet of thin white or coloured paper, and a soft pencil or wax crayon. A wax crayon is easier to use than a pencil on large surfaces because it covers more space and will not tear the paper.

Place the paper over the object and hold it down firmly with one hand. If the paper moves during the rubbing, the finished print will be blurred and spoilt.

Rub the pencil or crayon gently over the entire surface of the object. Continue to rub until the design shows through clearly. Make sure the rubbing is even. Light patches can be given an extra rub.

Fascinating subjects can be found out of doors. Make a collection of tree bark, fossil, stone, and leaf rubbings. Then mount them in a big nature scrap-book.

Take a new look at your street. Street name plates, ornamental manhole covers, commemoration plaques, and even brick walls can make good prints.

Brass Rubbings

Rubbings can also be taken from the ancient funerary brasses found in many churches and cathedrals. These brasses are set into the church floor or wall, and often depict knights in armour and ladies in long flowing medieval dresses.

Ask permission from someone in authority in the church or cathedral before starting to work. Sometimes they will ask for a fee, or grant permission only if an adult accompanies you. This is because the brasses are rare historic objects, and must be looked after carefully.

If a brass is large it may take several hours to complete a successful rubbing, so it is a good idea to take along a friend to assist with the work!

You will need a fairly large roll of paper. Lining paper is very suitable. Perhaps your father has some left over from decorating. It can also be bought at a painting and decorating shop.

Brass rubbings can be made with a wax crayon, but 'heelball' is the best rubbing medium to use. Heelball is a polish made from beeswax, tallow, and lamp black, and is used by cobblers. It is sold in some shoe repair shops, and art and craft shops.

To take a rubbing, start by carefully brushing away any dirt, dust or grit from the surface of the brass with a soft bristle brush and duster.

Place the paper in position on top of the brass and secure the edges of the paper with weights or books. Please do not use sticky tape to secure the paper to the brass, because it will leave behind little blobs of adhesive which can harm the surface of the brass. This technique can also be used on the beautiful lettering and carving found on ancient gravestones. In this case the paper is wrapped firmly round the stone and kept in position with masking tape (fig. 1). Masking tape can be bought at art and craft shops.

Nowadays in some English towns there are Brass Rubbing Centres. The centre is usually a church or hall which has a large collection of fibre-glass copies of old brasses. For a small fee, the centre provides all the necessary materials to work with and there are many splendid subjects to choose from.

fig. 1

2. Tie and Dye

Tie and dye is one of the earliest known methods of making patterns on cloth. It has been used in Japan, China, and India for over a thousand years.

The basic idea is very simple. Parts of a piece of cloth are bound up tightly with string or elastic bands, and the fabric is immersed in dye. The dye cannot penetrate the bindings, so that when the cloth is untied these areas remain the original colour, and the rest is dyed a new colour. Many patterns are made by tying the cloth in different ways.

Buy two tins of 'Dylon Cold Dye'. Choose bright colours such as red and yellow, or red and blue. You will also need two sachets of 'Dylon Cold Fix' or a packet of washing soda. These materials can be bought in chemists' shops and most large stores.

Find some old handkerchiefs or any fairly large scraps of material. If the material is brand new it must be washed to get rid of any chemical stiffening that might affect the dye and then left to dry.

The tying is done with thin waxed string or strong cotton thread. It is most important to pull the string as tightly as possible and to secure each binding with firm knots so that no dye can seep underneath and spoil the design.

Now turn to page 20 and read right to the end of the chapter before trying out the designs on the next two pages.

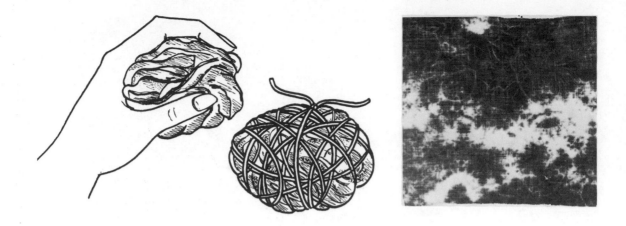

Marbling

This is an all-over design which looks a bit like marble. Crumple up the fabric in your hand and bind it round with string into a hard ball before dyeing. When dry, it can then be untied, crumpled again, rebound and dipped into a different-coloured dye.

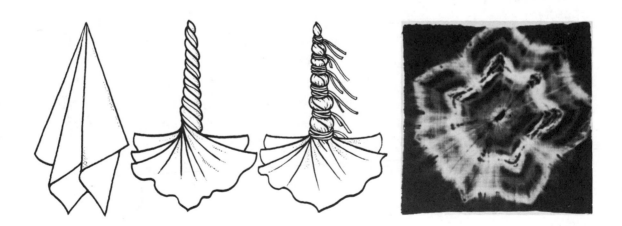

Sunburst

This makes a circular starry pattern of any size. Pick the fabric up at the point which is to be the centre of the circle and twist it round and round so that it looks like a furled umbrella. Bind it at intervals with string or elastic bands.

 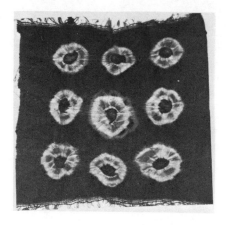

Small Circles

These can be made by covering little pebbles or dried beans and peas with fabric, and then tying string round them. If you want to make a pattern of circles, the easiest way is to mark the position of each circle centre on the material with a tiny pencil dot, and then to tie a pebble into the material at each of these points.

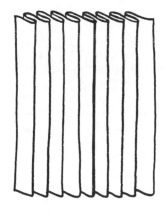  

Stripes

Pleating the fabric creates a striped design. Fold the material into a strip of accordion pleats and then bind it at intervals with string or elastic bands.

When the cloth has been tied, it is ready for dyeing. Follow the simple step-by-step instructions listed below.

Work in the kitchen and protect surfaces with newspaper. Wear old clothes and an apron. Rubber gloves are useful to protect hands.

Collect together a plastic bucket, a large basin or similar container to hold each dye, and some household salt.

Use the lightest-coloured dye first. Shake the dye powder into a container, and add 1 pint ($\frac{1}{2}$ litre) of warm water. Stir the solution until the powder dissolves. Add enough cold water to immerse the fabric.

Dissolve four tablespoons of household salt and one sachet of 'Dylon Cold Fix' (or one tablespoon of soda) in another pint ($\frac{1}{2}$ litre) of hot water. Add this solution to the dye and stir well.

Immerse the fabric in dye for at least one hour, then rinse it in clean water and hang up until completely dry.

Remove some of the bindings, and add extra ones. For example, if part of the pattern is to be kept the original colour of the fabric, it

must remain bound. Where a clear colour of the new dye is required, a piece of cloth must be untied to receive it.

Mix up the second dye and immerse the cloth for another hour. Dyes mix in the same way as paint-box colours, so that cloth dipped into red dye and then into blue will turn purple when the two colours merge. Hang the fabric up to dry, then untie it and iron smooth.

You can tie and dye with one colour, or as many as you like.

Use light colours first, and finish with the darkest colour.

First results of tie and dye are magical because the patterns seem to happen just by chance. Then with experience the method can be controlled to create exactly the type of pattern you want.

You will find this is an exciting way of decorating cotton clothes, such as a tee-shirt, old jeans, or the sleeves of a blouse. Try working on a large scale and make a wall hanging, cushion covers, or even curtains. Instructions enclosed with the dye powder explain how to dye large pieces of cloth in a washing machine.

3. Plaster Casting

Plaster is a soft white powder that can be mixed with water to form a creamy liquid. A chemical reaction takes place between the two substances and the mixture sets hard. Attractive tiles, wall plaques, brooches and pendants can be made by pouring the liquid plaster into clay moulds. When the plaster has set, the clay is peeled off and the resulting cast is painted.

To make a plaster cast you will need some plasticine or clay, plaster, and four lengths of wood of equal thickness, at least 1 in (2·5 cm) high. The best plaster to use is called 'Plaster of Paris', but other quick-setting types will work just as well. Plaster can be bought from Do-It-Yourself shops and hardware stores.

Cover the work surface with newspaper or polythene. Knead the clay so that it is evenly soft and flatten it out to form a slab about $\frac{1}{2}$ in (1·25 cm) thick. Use one of your pieces of wood as a straight edge and cut the slab into a square or rectangle (fig. 1).

Arrange the four pieces of wood around the slab of clay and hold them firmly in position with large blobs of clay (fig. 2). The diagram shows how the bits of wood can be adjusted to fit any square or rectangle. The depth inside the frame above the clay is to receive the liquid plaster.

The clay slab and the wood walls form the mould. Any lines or hollows cut into the clay will be reproduced as raised shapes on the plaster cast. To get an idea of how this works it is a good idea to make an experimental cast first, as shown in fig. 3.

All sorts of textures, lines and dots are scratched into the clay with a variety of instruments: the pointed end of a nail, a pin or a pencil. Small objects with interesting bumpy shapes such as a brooch, bottle tops, or the head of a screw can be pressed into the clay and then taken

22

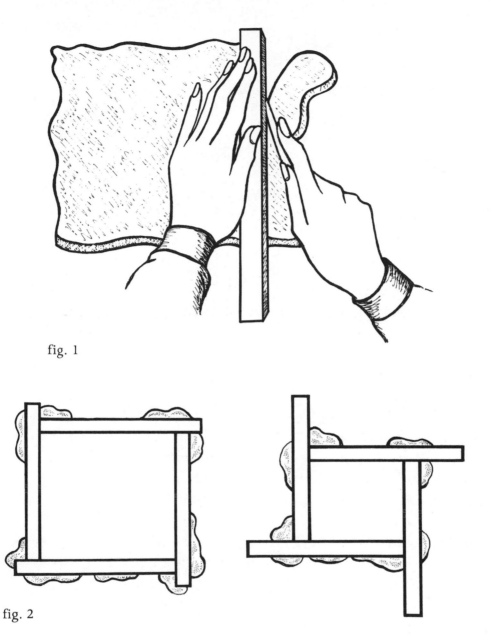

fig. 1

fig. 2

out to leave impressions. When the cast has been taken, you will be able to compare the different lines and textures and so get a clear idea of the enormous variety of effects that can be achieved.

When the mould is ready, mix up the plaster. Speed is essential because as soon as the plaster touches the water it starts to set.

Try to judge roughly how much liquid you will need to fill the

fig. 3

wooden frame up to the top, and pour this amount of cold water into a clean bowl. Quickly sprinkle plaster over the surface of the water. It will instantly sink to the bottom of the bowl. Continue sprinkling until the plaster begins to disappear more slowly and some blobs stay on the top, then mix it up with a spoon. The liquid should have the consistency of thin cream. If it is too thick, add more water and mix it in well.

Gently pour the plaster into the wooden frame, filling it to the top. Give the work surface a few knocks; this vibrates the plaster and makes sure that it runs into all the tiny crevices of the mould.

A small loop of wire or string can be pressed into the plaster (fig. 4). The loop will remain firmly in place when the cast is dry and can be used for hanging the finished object on the wall. If you are making a brooch, the clasp should be pressed into the plaster at this stage.

When the plaster feels hard, gently remove the pieces of wood and very carefully peel the slab of clay from the cast. It is interesting to see how everything that is done to the mould comes out in reverse on the cast. Lines scratched into the clay turn into sharp ridges, and

24

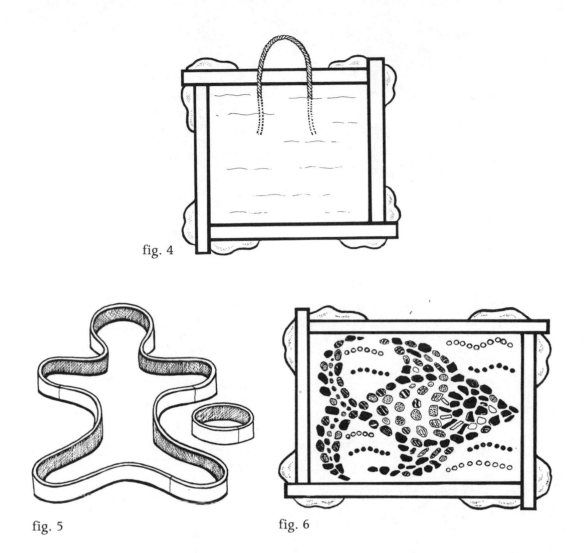

fig. 4

fig. 5

fig. 6

bumps of clay become hollows.

Leave the cast until it feels absolutely dry, then smooth down any rough edges with sandpaper and paint it with water-based paints or coloured inks (see the clown picture).

Left-over soft plaster in the bowl should be emptied into a waste bin, unless it can be used quickly to fill up another mould. Plaster must never be poured down the sink because it will block up the pipes. Instead of washing the bowl and spoon in the sink, allow the plaster to harden and then run cold water over them for a few seconds. The flakes

of plaster will rub off easily and can be thrown away.

All sorts of pictures and designs can be made by using and developing this basic method, as you will see from the drawings on page 26. Some of them have curved shapes; the walls of these casts are made of clay or plasticine instead of wood. The clay is cut into a long strip 1 in (2·5 cm) high, $\frac{1}{2}$ in (1·5 cm) thick, and bent into shape (fig. 5).

A Plaster Cast Mosaic

This is another way to make a decorative plaster cast. A clay mould is made in the usual way, and then buttons, small pebbles or beads are pressed half into the clay to make a simple mosaic pattern or picture (fig. 6). Plaster is poured into the mould and left to dry. When the clay is peeled off the cast, all the pebbles and beads will be imbedded in the plaster. If a few of the pieces drop out, they can be stuck back in with all-purpose clear glue. This would be a marvellous way of displaying a collection of unusual stones and shells picked up at the seaside. Do not make the mosaic plaque any bigger than 1 ft (31 cm) square; otherwise it will be very heavy and difficult to handle.

4. Papier-Mâché

Papier-mâché is another method of making a shape from a mould. Layers of damp paper are pasted one on top of the other and, when the paper is dry, the shape is taken off the mould and painted. Being very light in weight this material makes very good decorative boxes, bowls, trays, models, and all sorts of funny masks and hats.

You will need some newspaper, a small tin of vaseline (which can be bought from a chemist's shop), a bowl of water, paper paste, and a small stiff brush.

Use the cold water wall-paper paste that can be bought from a decorator's shop, or make your own, using 2 tablespoons of white flour and $\frac{3}{4}$ pint ($\frac{1}{2}$ litre) water. Mix the flour and some of the water to a smooth paste in a saucepan, add the remaining water, and stir well. Heat the saucepan gently until the paste thickens and bubbles, stirring all the time to prevent lumps, then pour the paste into a clean jar.

Next, choose a simple-shaped mould such as a small round bowl, tin tray, or plastic beaker. Avoid using very fragile china and objects that have complicated shapes.

If you use a bowl or beaker, rest it on top of a smaller object such as a jam jar to lift the sides of the mould free from the table (fig. 1). This makes the mould easier to handle when it is being covered with papier-mâché.

Rub a thin film of vaseline all over the outside of the mould to prevent the papier-mâché from sticking.

Tear the newspaper into strips roughly 1 in (2·5 cm) wide. Soak the strips in water for a few seconds, then remove them and gently squeeze out any surplus water so that they are damp instead of wet.

Beginning at the top of the mould, press on a strip of damp paper from the centre downwards so that at the bottom edge the paper

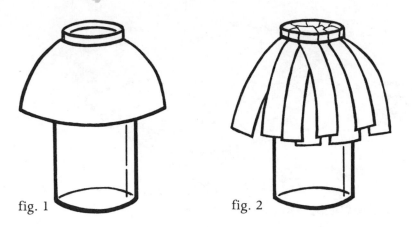

fig. 1   fig. 2

overhangs the mould. These overhanging pieces of paper will be trimmed off neatly later on. Add more strips of paper until the mould is covered (fig. 2). Don't worry if the paper does not stick to the vaseline very well; the second layer of paper and paste will anchor it down firmly. Brush lightly over with paste.

Now apply the second layer. Paste strips of paper on top of the first layer, tearing and arranging them as most convenient. The pieces of

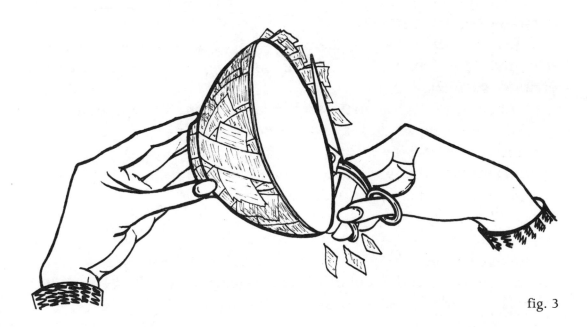

fig. 3

fig. 4

paper should overlap one another, because this gives strength to the finished article. When the mould is covered, brush the surface of the paper hard with plenty of paste to smooth out wrinkles and air bubbles.

Stick on seven more layers of paper in exactly the same way. Then leave the work to dry in a warm room: this may take a day or so.

When the papier-mâché feels really hard and dry, trim the overhanging pieces of paper flush to the edge of the mould (fig. 3). It should now be possible to ease the papier-mâché away from the mould. If the shape does not come off, run the blade of a blunt knife between the shape and the mould, then gently prise them apart. Any damage done with the knife can be patched up with paper and paste.

Neaten the edges of the shape by binding them with small pieces of damp pasted paper (fig. 4).

When the edges are dry, the papier-mâché is ready for decoration. Use any water-based paints and, if you like, finish off with a coat of shiny varnish.

Papier-mâché shapes can be stuck together with all-purpose adhesive to make amusing models like the ones in the picture, or to make decorative abstract sculptures. The shapes will suggest all sorts of exciting ideas to you. Extra additions such as hair, arms, and legs can be cut out of stiff paper and glued on.

Papier-maché Masks

To make a simple face mask that is tied on to the head with a loop of elastic or string, find a suitable-shaped mould that will fit over your face. This could be a shallow dish or baking tin.

30

Grease the mould with vaseline and cover it with six layers of papier-mâché, using the basic method already described.

When the shape has been removed from the mould, cut out two eye holes $1\frac{1}{2}$ in (4 cm) apart in the centre of the mask. Put the mask over your face just to make sure that the eye holes are big enough to see through. Pierce a small hole at either side of the mask for the strings to go into.

Decorate the mask in any fantastic way you like. Paint it or stick on cut-out paper shapes or found objects such as bits of wool, material, and shiny bottle tops. Cardboard cylinders and empty yoghourt cartons are very good for noses. Bushy beards, hair, eyebrows, and moustaches can be made from strips of material, or curled fringes of

paper. Try attaching some funny sticking-out ears and teeth made from thin card.

To make a mask that goes completely over the head, buy a large balloon from a toy shop, blow it up and rest it in a bowl (fig. 5).

Wrap damp strips of newspaper lengthways round the balloon, anchoring them down with small pieces of paper pasted on top (fig. 6).

Cover all the balloon, except the knot, with five layers of papier-mâché.

When the papier-mâché has dried, prick the balloon near the knot and remove it from the shape.

Enlarge the hole in the shape with scissors so that it is big enough to go over your head. Cut out holes for the eyes and nose (fig. 7).

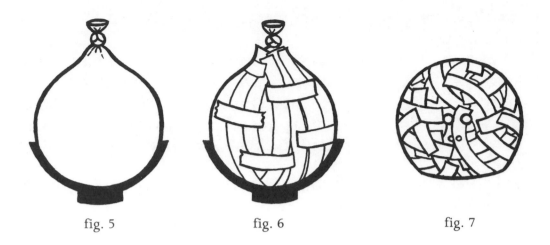

fig. 5   fig. 6   fig. 7

Now the mask can be decorated in any way you like. This balloon shape would make a marvellous spaceman's helmet, or it could be used to make all sorts of funny hats. Some ideas for hats and helmets are shown in the drawing.

5. Modelling with Wire

Wire comes in all sorts of thicknesses and colours. It can be twisted and bent into numerous shapes to make tiny or huge sculptures, decorations, twirling mobiles and delicate jewellery.

To work with wire, you will need a small pair of pointed-nosed pliers with a wire-cutting attachment.

It is important to buy soft wire that can be bent easily with pliers. The brightly coloured plastic-coated wire obtainable from electrical repair shops and large stores is good for first experiments. Galvanized wire is cheap and easily obtainable from hardware stores. It comes in different thicknesses called gauges; 18-gauge wire is suitable for most model work.

Always take care when you are working with wire, because the springy ends can sometimes fly up in the air and be a danger to eyes.

A Relief Decoration made from Wire

The attractive relief decoration shown on page 36 is really a picture drawn with wire. To make one, you will need stiff cardboard for the background and clear all-purpose glue.

The cardboard can be painted first or left its natural colour. Lightly draw the outline of the design you have in mind on to the card, keeping the shapes bold and simple.

Cut and bend pieces of wire to form the main shapes, following the pencil outline, and arrange them on the card: these shapes must be flat so that they will stick to the card. Build up the picture with more wire, and when it is complete, stick all the shapes on to the background with small blobs of glue.

Three-dimensional Models made from Wire

The basic method is to make a simple skeleton shape called an armature, then to wind more wire round it to build up the details.

Fig. 1 shows how an armature for a figure can be constructed in easy stages. The head, body and legs are made from one long piece of wire, with an extra strand twisted round the neck to make the arms. When the armature is finished, the limbs can be bent to give the figure movement. Extra wire is then coiled and twisted round the skeleton to build up the body shapes.

When the model is finished, it must be attached to a base so that it will stand up. Use a small block of balsa wood, plasticine, or cork for the base. These materials are sturdy but soft, so the sharp metal ends of the model can be pushed securely into them.

Fig. 2 shows how an armature for a four-legged animal can be constructed. The proportions of the head, body and legs will of course depend on the type of animal you want to make; for example, a giraffe will need a very long neck. Photographs will help you get the shapes of more unusual animals correct—you can also create strange monsters

36

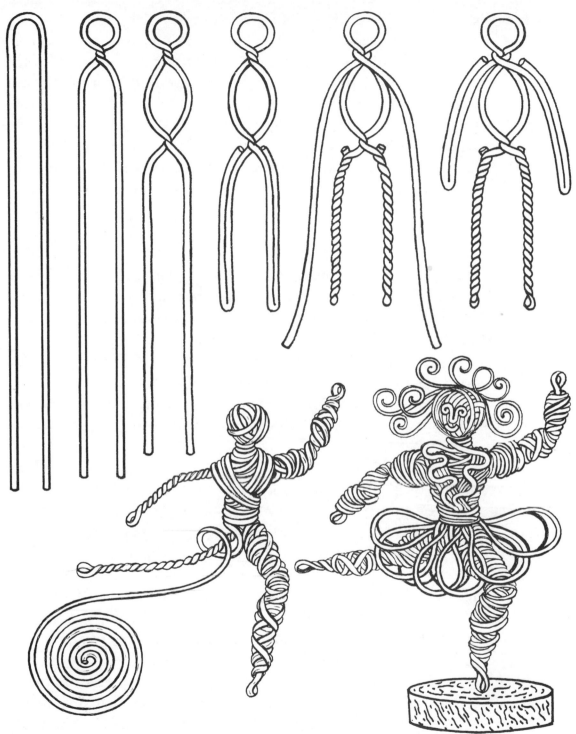

fig. 1

and dragons. Most four-legged animals will stand up by themselves, or they can be attached to a base like the figures.

When you have become more skilful at using wire, try creating some scenes that contain several figures and animals, perhaps with some delicate wire trees or a spiky castle in the background. There are lots of subjects that you could explore, such as an enchanted forest, a zoo or a moonscape.

The metallic colours of wire are very attractive, but if you want to make the models more colourful, they can be painted with the tiny tins of enamel paint available from craft shops or toy shops.

Models made from Wire and Papier-mâché
Another interesting way of making a model is to construct a simple wire armature, and then to cover it with papier-mâché.

When the armature is complete, tear up small strips of newspaper and soak them in paper paste. Cover the armature with at least three layers of paper, taking care to overlap the strips and smoothing them with a brush. Add extra layers of paper to the parts you want to make fatter. For very fine details use tissue paper instead of newspaper; this can be pressed into pointed shapes to make ears and noses and will dry quite hard.

When the model is dry, paint it with water-based paint. Try making clothes for figures out of paper or fabric. Make tails and manes for animals out of paper or string, and stick them on with clear all-purpose glue. Lots of other ideas for decorating the models will suggest themselves whilst you are working.

At some time you might want to make a giant-size model out of wire and papier-mâché. Large models are often very effective as theatrical props and in exhibition displays. Working on a large scale is exciting, particularly if some friends join in and help.

The basic technique is the same as for smaller models, except that chicken wire is used to make the armature. This is a wire mesh obtainable from hardware shops. It can be cut, bent or rolled into any shape. Several pieces bound together with soft wire make a strong but

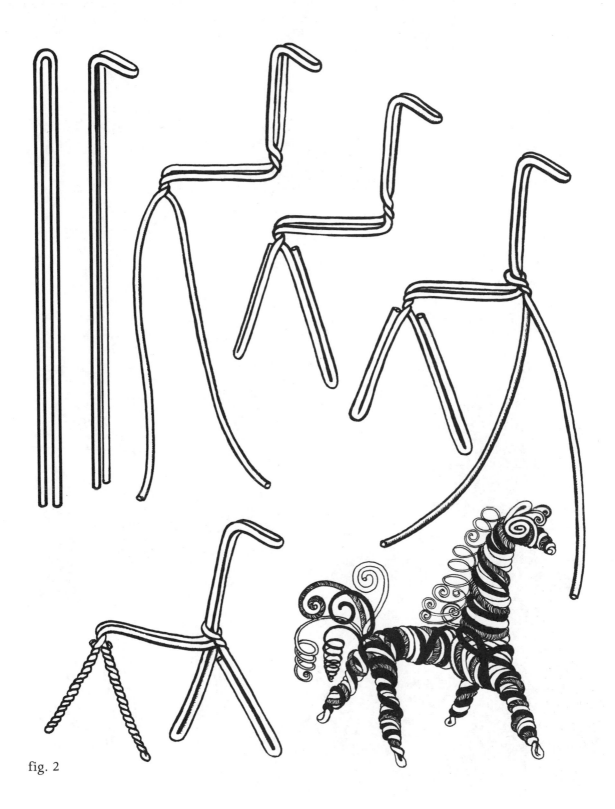

fig. 2

surprisingly light armature which can then be covered with papier-mâché and boldly painted. Wear gloves when handling chicken wire because the sharp ends can be scratchy.

Page 40 shows just a few more of the many fascinating things that can be made from wire. Try out ideas of your own and don't be afraid to experiment by combining different materials together to create unusual effects. Beads, feathers, tinsel; in fact almost anything can be tied or threaded on to wire or stuck to it with all-purpose clear glue.

6. Finger and Glove Puppets

Making a puppet can be just the beginning of an absorbing new hobby. If you want to put on a puppet play with some friends you will soon be involved in acting, thinking up plays, and painting scenery.

Finger Puppets

A simple paper finger puppet can be made in just a few minutes. Cut out a strip of paper about $2\frac{1}{2}$ in (6 cm) wide, roll it firmly round the top joint of your finger to make a cylinder, and then stick the edges of the paper together with all-purpose clear glue or sticky tape. Draw a funny face on the cylinder with a felt-tip pen, waggle your finger, and hey presto you have made a puppet!

Paper puppets are easily damaged. To make a more permanent finger puppet you can cut the fingers off an old glove or use scraps of felt. Small squares of felt can be bought in craft shops and large stores. Trace round fig. 1 and make a paper pattern, then use the pattern to cut out two shapes in felt. Use all-purpose glue to stick the shapes together round the edges, leaving the bottom open and enough room in the middle for your finger. Press the shapes together firmly to make sure that the glue sticks. Make faces by sticking on little bits of felt, paper, and fabric, or if you enjoy sewing, stitch on some woolly hair and embroider the face.

Glove Puppets

A glove puppet covers the whole hand. You can make a very amusing animal puppet from an old sock by sewing on two buttons to make eyes (fig. 2). Work by putting your thumb in the heel of the sock and fingers in the toe. To make the puppet look more realistic add woollen whiskers and felt ears, and stitch the toe to look like a nose (fig. 3).

fig. 1

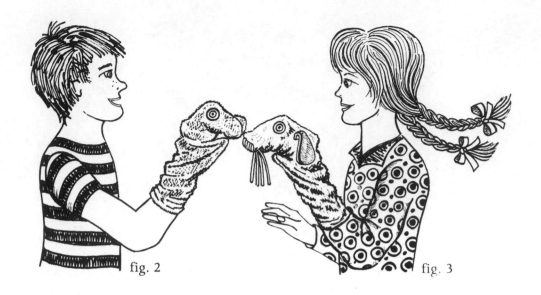

fig. 2   fig. 3

A Glove Puppet with a Papier-mâché Head

Model some clay or plasticine into a head shape on top of a stand. A bottle makes a good stand. The head should be as big as your fist, with a neck at least 2 in (5 cm) long. Eventually two of your fingers will go through the neck to control the head, so make sure that the neck is wide enough to take two fingers.

When the head is modelled, grease it well with vaseline. Then cover it with small strips of damp newspaper; the sticky vaseline will hold them in place. Brush lightly over with paste.

Paste six layers of papier-mâché on to the head. (Chapter 4 on papier-mâché will remind you of the basic method.) Use plenty of paste and brush the damp paper carefully into all the modelled details of the face.

When the head has dried out, trim round the bottom of the neck with a knife. Then beginning at the top of the head, cut down each side to the bottom of the neck to divide the head in two (fig. 4). Ease the two halves away from the mould. Stick them back together again with clear all-purpose glue and paste on a few strips of newspaper to strengthen and disguise the join.

Paint the head and, if you like, finish off with a coat of protective varnish. The hair and beards can be made from paper, strips of material, string or wool.

44

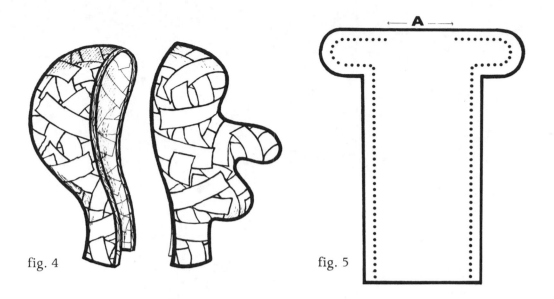

fig. 4   fig. 5

To make the glove you will need some strong cotton material. The simplest shape is the T-shaped bag shown in fig. 5. Make it wide enough to take your hand and long enough to reach half way down your forearm. The opening at the top of the bag (A in fig. 5) must be wide enough to receive the puppet's head. Draw a paper pattern first and then use it to cut out two shapes in material. Stitch the shapes together along the dotted lines shown in fig. 5, then turn the glove inside out to hide the stitching and iron it smooth.

Smear all-purpose clear glue round the neck of the puppet and insert it into the glove opening (A). Press the material on to the glue so that it sticks well. When the glue is dry, stitch the glove strongly on either side of the neck to strengthen the puppet at the points where it receives the most wear.

The glove can be decorated with paint, scraps of material, buttons and braid. Or if you want the puppet to have several costumes to suit the parts it is playing, you can make over-dresses. These dresses are just simple oblong bags with openings for the arms and head (fig. 6). The puppet head will be too large to go through the neck of the dress, so put the dress on 'feet first' by pushing the bottom of the glove through the neck hole of the dress.

45

fig. 6

A simple puppet stage can be made by turning a table on its side, or by tying a broomstick between the tops of two chairs and draping an old sheet between them. Sit behind the sheet or table and hold the puppet up over the top. A table lamp makes a good spot-light. If you become interested in puppetry you will probably want to build a more permanent puppet theatre. Your local library should have detailed books on the subject which will show you how to make a theatre and also give you many other interesting ideas.

fig. 1

7. Collage

A collage is a picture which hasn't been drawn or painted. It is built up from pieces of paper, cloth, or any other materials which are glued or sewn on to a background.

Paper Collage

Perhaps you have already made a collage out of paper; if not you will find it very easy and a lot of fun. You will need a large sheet of paper for the background, some old magazines, and any scraps of patterned or plain coloured paper that can be found, including paper bags, glue, pencil and scissors.

Think of an interesting subject—this could be anything from a jolly fat lady to a jungle scene. Cut out the main shapes and arrange them on the background. Make use of the wide variety of textures and patterns that can be found in magazines; for example, the fat lady could have a dress cut from a photograph of a checked table-cloth, and wear some flowers cut out of a gardening picture on her hat. Stick all the shapes on to the background, add any extra little details, and the picture is complete.

Photo Collage

Fig. 1 shows a photo collage. This is a paper collage but all the parts of the picture are cut out of photographs found in magazines and newspapers. The results can be very amusing, so why not have a competition with some friends and see who can make the funniest face?

Fabric Collage

Collect together as many different scraps of material as possible, but make sure that your mother's favourite table-cloth has not been included!

You will also need a fairly large piece of strong cloth for the background. Cut it to shape, making sure that the woven threads go straight down and across (fig. 2). Iron the material smooth and lay it on the table.

A fabric collage can be quickly made by cutting out the shapes from scraps of material, ironing them smooth and sticking them on the background with a suitable glue (Copydex or any all-purpose glue). Spread the glue sparingly on the back of each shape round the edges and press them firmly into position. If too much glue is used, it can soak through the material and leave stains.

When arranging and cutting out the shapes, use the texture of the fabrics to their best advantage. A dog will look more hairy if it is cut out of thick woolly material, whilst shiny satin would be more suitable for a river. Strange misty effects can be achieved by sticking transparent fabrics such as net and organdie over the top of other shapes. Lace, braid, strands of wool, buttons, sequins and beads can all be stuck or sewn on to the picture to give detail and extra richness.

If you can sew, try stitching the shapes into position instead of sticking them. This is a more permanent way of making a collage, but it takes longer.

Here are a few sewing hints.

As far as possible the threads of the fabric should go straight down and across each shape (fig. 2). This stops them stretching and puckering up when they are sewn on to the background.

Some pieces of loosely woven material start to fray when they are cut out. This means that the woven threads round the edges pull out. If this happens, turn a small hem on to the wrong side of the fabric all round the edge of the shape and sew it down with small stitches (fig. 3). On thicker materials such as tweed a hem would look very bumpy; instead lightly smear glue round the edges of the shape on the underside, which sticks the threads together and stops them falling out.

Arrange the shapes on the cloth, pin and tack them into position. 'Tacking' means roughly sewing them down with large stitches which

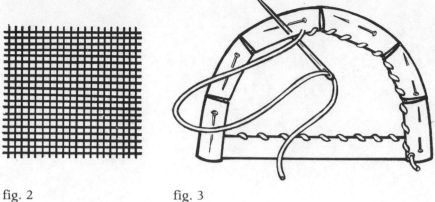

fig. 2   fig. 3

are removed later.

Sew the shapes on to the background, using either tiny stitches that cannot be seen, or big bold stitches that become part of the design. Some bits of the picture could be embroidered with brightly coloured wool.

Finally, remove all the pins and tacking stitches, and press with a damp cloth on the back of the picture. Pin the collage on the wall, or lightly glue it on to a piece of stiff card. A collage that is well sewn down could also be made into a cushion cover.

A more unusual way of displaying the collage would be to mount it behind an old picture frame. Attractive frames can often be bought very cheaply from jumble sales, or perhaps there is one stored away at home. Clean it up and if necessary give it a coat of fresh paint. Ask your parents or teacher to help you fit the collage into the frame.

Collages made out of paper and fabric have been described here, but there are many other things to use in the same way. The wire picture on page 36 is an example of a collage made from another material. Try an arrangement of pressed flowers and leaves, dried peas and beans, or even pieces of macaroni!

Technique B (see page 60).

8. Experiments with Photography

Printing a photograph from a negative does not require special equipment or knowledge; it is a straightforward job that can be carried out at home. There are also other ways of creating photographic pictures without using a negative or even a camera.

This is how the photographic printing process works: photographic paper has a special glossy coating on one side that is very sensitive to light. If any light falls on the sensitive coating, an invisible chemical reaction takes place. When the paper is treated with two chemical solutions called developer and fixer ('printed') it turns from white to black.

Imagine that a small cardboard circle is placed on the sensitive paper in total darkness, and it is then exposed to light. Afterwards the circle is removed and the paper is printed. The result will be a black sheet of paper with a white circle on it. This is because the cardboard shape has stopped the light rays from penetrating the sensitive paper underneath it, so no chemical reaction takes place, and that piece of paper remains white.

A photographic negative works in the same way as the shape; if it is placed on top of a piece of sensitive paper, the black areas block out the light, clear areas let the light through and grey areas allow some of the light to penetrate. When the paper is developed the result is a black and white photograph containing shades of grey. From this you will realise that making a photographic image is really a fascinating way of painting with light.

It is more fun if you can work with a few friends, since extra help is useful during the photographic printing process, and you can share the cost of essential materials and equipment.

Buy the following equipment from a photographic shop: a bottle of

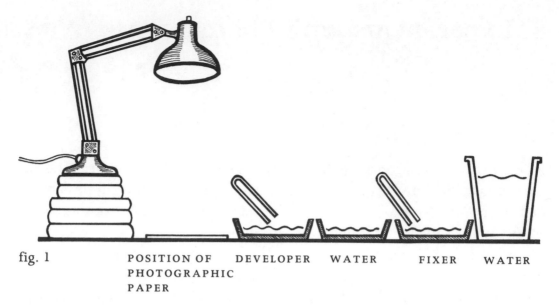

fig. 1   POSITION OF   DEVELOPER   WATER   FIXER   WATER
PHOTOGRAPHIC
PAPER

developer and a bottle of fixer suitable for use with bromide paper; two pairs of plastic tongs; a packet of single or double weight bromide photographic paper. (10 in × 8 in [25 cm × 20 cm] is a good size to start off with.) ALWAYS REMEMBER THAT THIS PAPER MUST NOT BE OPENED IN THE LIGHT.

You will also need: a sheet of clean glass a little larger than the photographic paper; a safelight (a torch with red glass or red cellophane wrapped round it—a dim red light does not affect the sensitive photographic paper); a table lamp with a low-power light bulb and a hand switch; three shallow dishes as shown in fig. 1 (the dishes must not be made of metal because the chemicals can corrode them; plastic seed boxes work well).

Step 1 Arranging the Equipment
Photographic printing must be carried out in total darkness. Therefore choose a room with thick curtains and work at night. Fig. 1 shows how the lamp and dishes are arranged. The light bulb should be at least 2 ft (60 cm) above the table with the beam shining directly downwards.

It is essential that the lamp light should shine evenly on to the piece of photographic paper. To ensure this place a sheet of ordinary white

56

paper on the table directly underneath the lamp and switch off any other lights in the room. If there is a bright spot in the middle of the paper or any darkening round the edges, adjust the lamp until they disappear.

Step 2 Mixing the Chemicals
Take great care when you are mixing up the chemicals because they can stain clothes and irritate the skin.

Into the first dish, put some of the developing solution mixed according to the instructions on the label. It should be at a temperature of about 65° Fahrenheit. This is normal living-room temperature, so if you leave the bottle and a jug of water in the living room during the day, they should be just the right temperature for use at night.

In the second dish put some clean water, and in the third dish the fixing solution mixed up according to instructions. Lastly, fill up a large bowl with water.

Step 3 Taking a Test Strip
Before starting your first photographic print, it is a good idea to make a test strip. This is a way of calculating how much light (exposure time) is required to make a good print.

Make sure that the packet of photographic paper, scissors and a book are on the table. Switch off the lights. The room must be in total darkness except for the red glow of the safelight. It is a good idea to warn the rest of the family that you are starting work so that they don't suddenly open the door and flood the room with light.

Open the packet of photographic paper, cut a 2 in (5 cm) strip off a sheet and place it glossy side upwards on the table directly beneath the lamp. Return the remainder of the sheet to the packet. Close the packet carefully and put it in a place where it will be protected from the light.

With a book, cover the strip except for 2 in (5 cm) at the top (fig. 2). Switch on the lamp, count one and then move the book down to expose another 2 in (5 cm) of paper on the count of two. Continue to count in seconds, exposing a bit more of the paper each time until the whole strip is exposed. Switch off the lamp.

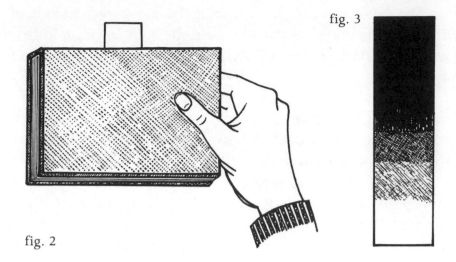

fig. 3

fig. 2

Place the paper in the developer. The solution must cover the paper. Using tongs, move the paper about and watch for black areas to appear. After two minutes remove the paper with tongs and rinse it in clean water.

Finally, place the paper in the fixing solution, using the second pair of tongs. Separate tongs are used with the fixer and developer, to make sure that the chemicals do not mix together and stain the prints.

Leave the print in the solution until it is properly fixed according to instructions. The light can be switched on when the print has been in the fixer for two minutes. Before switching on the lights, see that the rest of the photographic paper is safely inside its light-proof packet and stored away.

Examine the test strip: the part that was exposed for the longest time will be very black and the other end will be paler (fig. 3). Find the first section of the strip that has turned a rich black and count how many seconds it was exposed to the light. You will use this exposure time for your pictures.

If the test strip goes completely black, the exposures were too long with this strength of light, so use a weaker bulb in the table lamp and take another test. If the strip was very pale, the exposures were too short. Take another test strip, counting two seconds for each exposed 2 in (5 cm) of paper.

Technique C (see page 60).

Step 4 Making Pictures

Here are some fascinating ways of making photographic pictures; in each case the pictures are exposed to the light for the amount of time determined by the test strip and then developed and fixed in the same way.

A. Cut out shapes from thick paper or card and arrange them into a picture. In darkness (red safelight on), place a sheet of photographic paper glossy side up, underneath the lamp. Then transfer the shapes (keeping the same arrangement) on top of the photographic paper, and lay a sheet of glass over them both. Expose, and print the picture. The cut shapes will produce white images against a black background. If you want to produce the same picture with black shapes on a white background, dry the first print, then place it face down on top of a new piece of photographic paper and lay the sheet of glass on top. Expose and print it as before. Believe it or not, this does work.

B. In darkness (red safelight on), make an arrangement on the photographic paper (glossy side up) using other things that will block out the light such as pieces of string, lace, leaves and grasses. Expose and print the picture as above.

C. Paint a picture on to the sheet of glass with very thick orange poster paint. When it is dry, with the red safelight on only, place the picture on top of the photographic paper (glossy side up), expose and print.

D. Cover the sheet of glass with a thick layer of orange paint. When the paint is dry, hold the glass up to the light to make sure that the paint is even and that no light is getting through. Scratch a drawing through the paint with a darning needle or any other pointed instrument. In darkness except for red safelight, place the glass on top of a sheet of photographic paper (glossy side up), expose and print the picture. If you have a piece of old blackened photographic negative, you can scratch a drawing on one side in the same way.

E. Take a print from a photographic negative. In darkness except for red safelight, place the negative on the photographic paper (glossy

Technique A (see page 60).

Technique D (see page 60).

side up) and lay a sheet of glass on top. Expose and print the picture.

Step 5 Finishing Off

After fixing, all your prints need to be washed in clean water for half an hour.

To dry the prints, gently sponge off any excess moisture and lay them down on a clean flat surface.

The prints may curl up a bit when they are dry, so press them flat between some heavy books.

These instructions may sound complicated, but once you get started they are quite simple and quick to carry out, and the results are very exciting.

Technique B (see page 60).

Acknowledgements

The two brass rubbings on page 15 are reproduced by courtesy of Faber and Faber Ltd. from *Monumental Brasses: the Craft* by Malcolm Norris.

DATE DUE

1-17-80			
JAN 2 7 1981			
FEB 1 7 1981			
MAR 1 0 1981			
MAR 2 4 1981			
1-18-82			
FEB 1 2 1984			
JUN 1 8 1984			
11-27-84			
NOV 2 6 19__			
MAR 3 1986			
MAY 2 4 1988			
FEB 0 1 1989			
JUN 0 6 1989			
MAY 1 1 1998			
MAY 1 8 1999			
MAR 0 7 2000			

GAYLORD   PRINTED IN U.S.A.